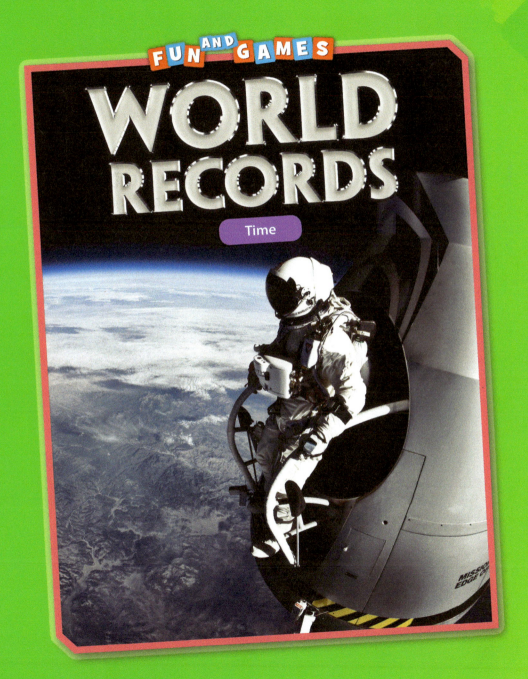

# FUN AND GAMES
# WORLD RECORDS
## Time

Elise Wallace

## Consultants

**Michele Ogden, Ed.D**
Principal
Irvine Unified School District

**Colleen Pollitt, M.A.Ed.**
Math Support Teacher
Howard County Public Schools

## Publishing Credits

Rachelle Cracchiolo, M.S.Ed., *Publisher*
Conni Medina, M.A.Ed., *Managing Editor*
Dona Herweck Rice, *Series Developer*
Emily R. Smith, M.A.Ed., *Series Developer*
Diana Kenney, M.A.Ed., NBCT, *Content Director*
Stacy Monsman, M.A., *Editor*
Kevin Panter, *Graphic Designer*

**Image Credits:** Cover and p.1 Jay Nemeth/ZUMA Press/Newscom; p.4 Ben Stansall/AFP/Getty Images; pp.6–7 PA Images/Alamy Stock Photo; p.8 The Advertising Archives/Alamy Stock Photo; p.9 Courtesy of Owen Larsen; p.10 WENN Ltd/Alamy Stock Photo; pp.10–11 Jonathan Hordle/Rex Features via AP Images; p.12 Paul Drinkwater/NBC/NBCU Photo Bank via Getty Images; pp.12, 13 Paul Drinkwater/NBC/NBCU Photo Bank via Getty Images; p.14 Courtesy of Mischo Erban; pp.14–15 Ezra Shaw/Getty Images; pp.16–17 Nigel Hicks/Alamy Stock Photo; p.17 (top) PA Images/Alamy Stock Photo, (bottom) Jean-Sebastien Evrard/AFP/Getty Images; pp.18,18–19 Courtesy of Lucas Wilson; pp.22–23 ZUMA Press/ZUMAPRESS/Newscom; pp.22 (top) Jay Nemeth/ZUMA Press/Newscom; p.23 EDB Image Archive/Alamy Stock Photo; pp.24–25 leonello calvetti/Alamy Stock Photo; p.25 Michael Liebrecht/Alamy Stock Photo; p.26 Christopher Ison/Alamy Stock Photo; p.27 (top) PA Images/Alamy Stock Photo, (bottom) Brian Hickey Photography/Alamy Stock Photo; p.31 Antony Nettle/Alamy Stock Photo; all other images from iStock and/or Shutterstock.

### Library of Congress Cataloging-in-Publication Data

Names: Wallace, Elise, author.
Title: Fun and games : world records / Elise Wallace.
Description: Huntington, Beach, CA : Teacher Created Materials, 2018. | Includes index. | Audience: Grade 4 to 6.
Identifiers: LCCN 2017012137 (print) | LCCN 2017037550 (ebook) | ISBN 9781480759404 (eBook) | ISBN 9781425855581 (pbk.)
Subjects: LCSH: Speed records--Juvenile literature. | Time--Juvenile literature.
Classification: LCC GV1019 (ebook) | LCC GV1019 .W35 2018 (print) | DDC 796.1--dc23
LC record available at https://lccn.loc.gov/2017012137

**Teacher Created Materials**
5301 Oceanus Drive
Huntington Beach, CA 92649-1030
http://www.tcmpub.com

**ISBN 978-1-4258-5558-1**
© 2018 Teacher Created Materials, Inc.

# Table of Contents

Making Record Time ............................................4

By Land .................................................................7

By Water ............................................................ 16

By Air ................................................................. 23

Time to Beat ...................................................... 26

Problem Solving ................................................ 28

Glossary ............................................................. 30

Index .................................................................. 31

Answer Key ....................................................... 32

# Making Record Time

Ready? Set? Go! It's time to explore some of the most amazing races in the world. Ever heard of piggyback racing? How about speed skydiving? Participants in these competitions hope to set new world **records**. They will do anything to achieve their goals. These are their stories.

You will meet a lot of interesting people trying to be the best in their field. You'll meet people like Edd China. He is the brains behind the fastest toilet in the world. You'll also meet furry friends like Sweet Pea, a talented pup. Sweet Pea set the record for walking the fastest 100 meters (328 feet) *while* balancing a soda can.

Inventor Edd China races the world's fastest toilet in London.

These adventurous **competitors** will take us from land to sea. They will take us from open fields to great heights. The competitions may seem silly. But, the participants are serious. Each of them has worked hard to make record **time**. Hold on tight. It's sure to be an interesting ride.

A skydiver free falls from an airplane before pulling his parachute.

## LET'S EXPLORE MATH

Selena and Adam are designing races for a class competition. They need to select **units** to measure the time it takes to finish each race.

1. Is it better to measure the time it takes to hop around the classroom in minutes or hours? Explain your reasoning.
2. Is it better to measure the time it takes to write your name in minutes or seconds? Explain your reasoning.

Usain Bolt competes in the men's 200-meter final at the 2013 World Athletics Championships.

# By Land

You've probably heard the names of some of the fastest people in the world. Usain Bolt is a sprinter. Apolo Ohno is a speed skater. These athletes are masters of their sports. They are heroes to many.

There are many other lightning-quick competitors out there. Some of them have broken world records. Some of them have set new records by creating their own contests. Either way, they aren't all star athletes. Some of them are inventors. Some of them have talented pets. The possibilities are endless!

Apolo Ohno competes in short-track speed skating at the 2010 Winter Olympics in Canada.

# An Unlikely Race

In 2015, a new record was set on land; two young men set the record for piggyback racing! Owen Larsen ran the fastest mile *while* carrying Jordan Botwright on his back. He didn't drop his partner once!

Both men are from the United Kingdom. They are members of a British **regiment** known for training skilled soldiers. They fought in the Middle East with their troops. Larsen and Botwright ran the mile to raise money. They wanted to support a national charity that provides help to British soldiers and veterans.

It took Larsen 11 **minutes** and 11 **seconds** to complete the mile. Not bad, considering he was running laps while carrying his buddy on his back!

This flyer advertises the UK Army Benevolent Fund, the charity supported by Larsen and Botwright.

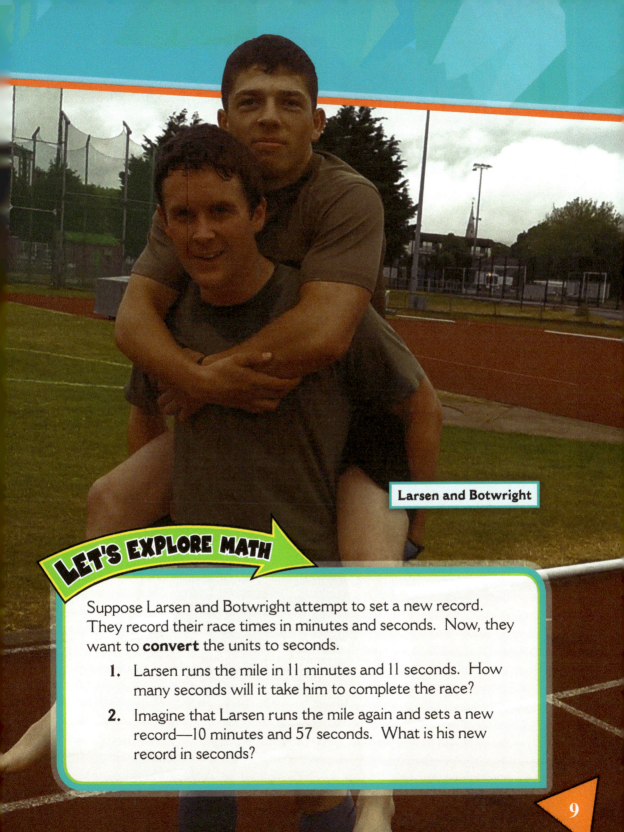

Larsen and Botwright

## LET'S EXPLORE MATH

Suppose Larsen and Botwright attempt to set a new record. They record their race times in minutes and seconds. Now, they want to **convert** the units to seconds.

1. Larsen runs the mile in 11 minutes and 11 seconds. How many seconds will it take him to complete the race?

2. Imagine that Larsen runs the mile again and sets a new record—10 minutes and 57 seconds. What is his new record in seconds?

## Toilet Racing

The fastest toilet in the world has a name. It is known as the *Bog Standard*. The driver behind the toilet has a name, too. His name is Edd China. He set the racing record in Milan, Italy, in 2011.

You might be asking yourself how he races on a toilet. After all, toilets don't have wheels. Well, that didn't stop China. China is an inventor. He built the toilet out of a motorcycle and sidecar. The vehicle includes a toilet, a bathtub, a sink, *and* a laundry bin. The sink is what steers the machine! The toilet reached a speed of 68 kilometers per **hour** (42 miles per hour). China set this record wearing a sport coat and racing goggles.

A rival built a racing toilet in 2013. His name is Colin Furze. He claims his toilet can reach 85 kph (53 mph). He even tried to beat China's record. But for now, China is still the top toilet racer.

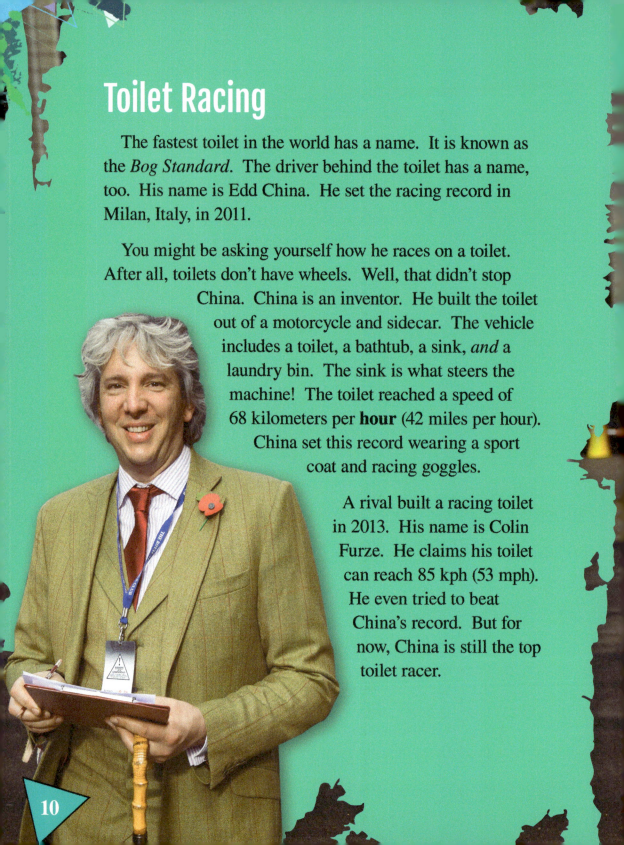

Edd China gives a passenger a ride around London in his invention.

11

# Doggone Fun

Sweet Pea is a one-of-a-kind pooch. She is a border collie-Australian shepherd mix. She also holds not one, not two, but three records! Alex Rothacker is Sweet Pea's trainer and owner. He taught her the art of balance. He knew she could achieve great things.

Sweet Pea set all three of her world records in 2008. First, she set the record for the fastest 100 m (328 ft.) while balancing a soda can on her head. Her time was 2 minutes and 55 seconds.

But Sweet Pea set another record. She walked down 10 stairs facing forward. Then, she walked backward up the stairs. She did it all while balancing a 5-ounce glass of water on her head! That added two new records to her name.

Rothacker is proud of his talented pup. He says, "You can teach a dog anything, it just takes time."

Sweet Pea

Sweet Pea balances a glass of water on her head.

## LET'S EXPLORE MATH

Peter is training his border collie, Bailey, for an upcoming dog show. He takes Bailey to a local farm to practice herding sheep. He records the number of hours and minutes he trains Bailey over the first three days. He creates a **conversion table** to write the times in minutes and seconds.

1. Complete the table below.
2. Are there more minutes or seconds in an hour? Show your thinking.

| Day | Time in Hours | Time in Minutes | Time in Seconds |
|---|---|---|---|
| 1 | 2 hrs. 15 min. | 135 min. | 8,100 sec. |
| 2 | 1 hr. 25 min. | 85 min. | |
| 3 | 1 hr. 10 min. | | 4,200 sec. |

# Fastest Electric Skateboard

Meet Mischo Erban. He welcomes danger. Erban holds the title for fastest speed on an electric skateboard.

Erban's record run was in 2016 on an airport runway. The runway provided him with a flat surface. It helped give him a smoother run. To protect his body, he wore special clothing. His bodysuit and helmet kept him safe during his run.

He controlled his skateboard with a remote during the run. Erban reached speeds up to 96 kph (60 mph). But then, he lost control and crashed. Luckily, he was unharmed. And, he set the record before he fell! Despite his fall, Erban continues to race. He says, "I am attracted by speed and have learned to master the danger."

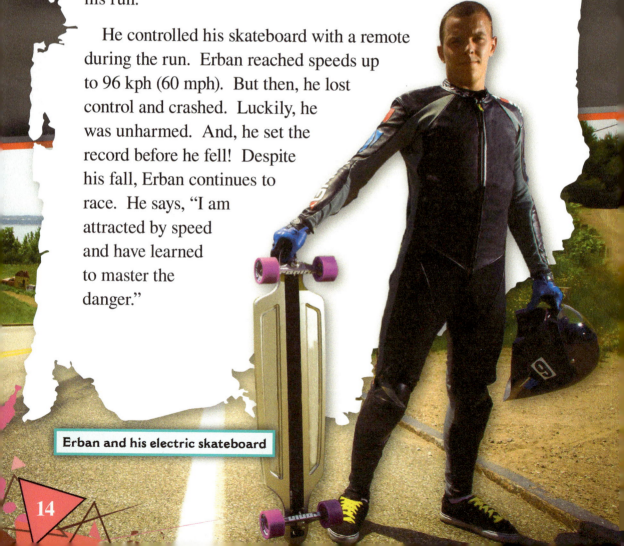

Erban and his electric skateboard

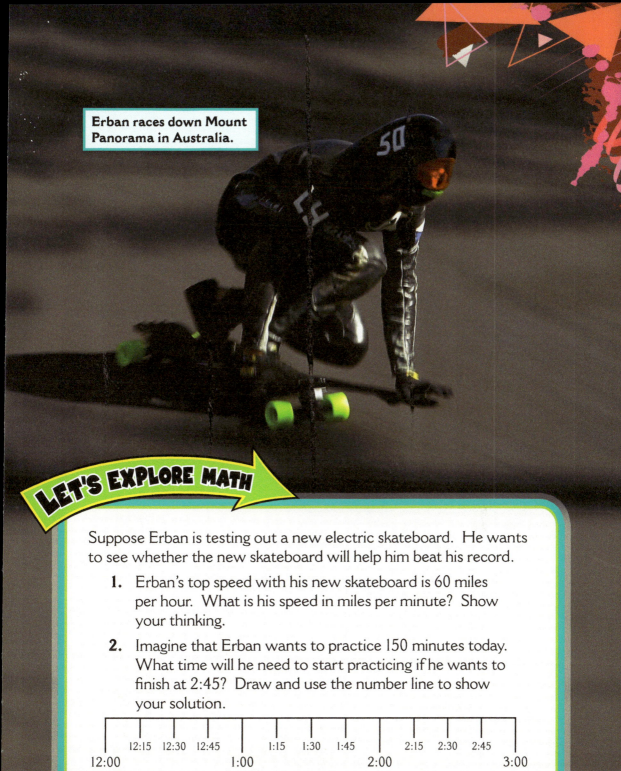

Erban races down Mount Panorama in Australia.

## LET'S EXPLORE MATH

Suppose Erban is testing out a new electric skateboard. He wants to see whether the new skateboard will help him beat his record.

1. Erban's top speed with his new skateboard is 60 miles per hour. What is his speed in miles per minute? Show your thinking.

2. Imagine that Erban wants to practice 150 minutes today. What time will he need to start practicing if he wants to finish at 2:45? Draw and use the number line to show your solution.

# By Water

These next competitors hold **aquatic** records. They zip and zoom across rivers, lakes, and oceans. They sail and swim through crashing waves. These are the fastest people on water.

## Sailing Around the World

Ellen MacArthur is a British sailor. She has set many records. In 2005, MacArthur set her greatest record. At 28, she sailed around the world. She began her voyage in France. First, she sailed to the Cape of Good Hope. Then, she traveled south of Australia. From there, she sailed past Cape Horn. Finally, she sailed across the Atlantic and returned to France. She had done it! MacArthur was the fastest person to circle the globe by sail.

MacArthur sails a yacht off the coast of Great Britain.

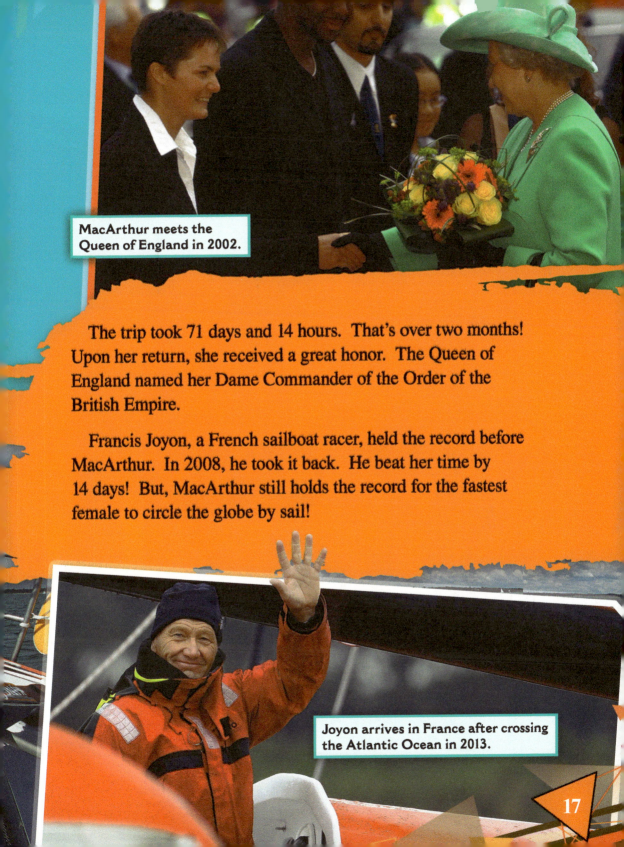

MacArthur meets the Queen of England in 2002.

The trip took 71 days and 14 hours. That's over two months! Upon her return, she received a great honor. The Queen of England named her Dame Commander of the Order of the British Empire.

Francis Joyon, a French sailboat racer, held the record before MacArthur. In 2008, he took it back. He beat her time by 14 days! But, MacArthur still holds the record for the fastest female to circle the globe by sail!

Joyon arrives in France after crossing the Atlantic Ocean in 2013.

# Underwater Escape Artist

Lucas Wilson has special skills. He can free himself from chains. He can outsmart straitjackets while hanging upside down. He can even escape from a straitjacket while underwater! In other words, Wilson is an escape artist. He tries to do the impossible in record time.

Every year, there is a televised stunt show in Italy. It shows people attempting strange **feats**. In 2014, Wilson was on the show. Being filmed while trying a stunt might be scary for some people. But underwater escapes aren't new for Wilson. In fact, he wasn't trying to break someone else's record. Wilson was trying to break his own.

Despite the pressure, Wilson was successful. He escaped in just under 23 seconds. He broke his last record by fractions of a second. Wilson also broke two other records. He performed two escape acts while **suspended** by his ankles. Three world records! Well done, Wilson.

Wilson attempts to escape from a straitjacket while upside down.

Wilson escapes from a straitjacket while underwater.

# Swimming Sensations

Swimming was a hobby in many ancient empires, from Greece to Japan. In 1896, it became an Olympic sport. Women's swimming was recognized as an Olympic sport in 1912.

One of the most famous American swimmers is Michael Phelps. He was very active as a child. He started to swim as a way to get rid of his energy. It paid off. Phelps set his first world record when he was only 15 years old. Since then, he has won 28 Olympic medals, of which 23 are gold!

Michael Phelps

Phelps competes in the 200-meter individual medley at the 2016 Olympics in Brazil.

Ledecky competes in the 800-meter freestyle at the 2016 Olympics in Brazil.

Katie Ledecky is also an American swimmer who has won Olympic gold. What makes her unique? She won four gold medals in the same event! She is one of only three women to have done this. She is also known for breaking records—even her own! She has set 12 world records. When she's not in the pool, she likes to play games like Scrabble© and chess.

Katie Ledecky

Baumgartner prepares to jump from a capsule 29,455 meters (18 miles) above Earth.

Baumgartner free falls at record speed.

# By Air

They surf the skies. They fly at record speeds. These are the thrill-seekers and daredevils of the air!

## Speed Skydiving

Felix Baumgartner has always had a love for the extreme. He started skydiving at the age of 16. In his 20s, he began BASE jumping. BASE jumpers jump from buildings rather than planes. It is much more dangerous. It is also much more extreme! Baumgartner has 14 world records for BASE jumps he completed all over the world.

In 2012, he became the first human to go faster than the speed of sound in free fall. He climbed to 39,045 m (128,100 ft.) in a special balloon. He fell at a speed of 1,342 kph (834 mph). Imagine falling that fast! He spent just over four minutes in free fall. Then, he pulled his parachute. The entire trip was less than 10 minutes!

This jump was for more than the thrill. The data gathered from his jump will help the National Aeronautics and Space Administration (NASA). NASA can use this data for future space exploration.

## Fastest Commercial Flight

When people think of fast aircraft, they often think of jets and rockets. But, the Concorde was neither. It was a commercial airplane. That's the kind of plane people take when they go on vacation with their families. The planes are big and bulky. They are not known for their speed.

But, the Concorde wasn't an average aircraft. Even though it was a commercial airplane, it was built for speed. The first Concorde took flight in 1969. But it took almost a decade for the airplane to begin taking regular passengers.

From the start, the Concorde was fast. The plane could reach 2,173 kph (1,350 mph). That's more than twice the speed of sound! Such speed drastically cuts travel times. When the Concorde broke the record for the fastest commercial flight in 1996, the passengers were surprised. They had not known that they were making history!

## LET'S EXPLORE MATH

Concorde reached its top speed of 2,173 kilometers per hour in 1996. How many meters per hour did it travel? Show your thinking.

Concorde lands in Germany.

# Time to Beat

We all want to make our mark on the world. We want to do something fantastic. We hope to reach new heights. If setting a world record is one of your goals, it's time to start thinking about which record you want to beat. But remember, you want your record to be official. So, be sure to apply for a record and get it verified. There's nothing worse than setting an unofficial record. Imagine all of that hard work with zero payoff!

If you're having trouble knowing where to start, ask yourself a few questions. What are my strengths? Do I excel on land, water, or in the air? Do I want to set a record in something silly and strange? Or, do I want to set a more traditional record? Once you set your sights on a goal, start training. You just might be the next Ellen MacArthur or Michael Phelps!

At 100 years of age, Doris Long breaks her own record for being the world's oldest person to use a rope to slide down a 130-meter tall building.

Alastair Moffat celebrates after parallel parking a car in the world's tightest space.

Mustapha Danger sets a new world record for riding a motorcycle across a 1,640-foot tightrope without a safety net.

# Problem Solving

Imagine you are sailing across the Atlantic Ocean. You want to beat the world record. You know it's a long journey, but just how long will it take? There are 3,600 miles between you and the finish line.

1. You make it halfway across the Atlantic Ocean. If your average speed is 5 miles per hour, how many hours does it take you?

2. You lose time in a storm. Your boat hasn't moved in two days! How many hours have you traveled since the beginning of the trip? (Hint: Use your answer from the previous question to help you solve this problem.)

3. You are picking up speed. You average 10 miles per hour during the second half of your trip. How many hours does the second half of the trip take?

4. You've sailed across the Atlantic! It took you 18 days and 6 hours to complete your voyage. How many hours did your journey take?

# Glossary

**aquatic**—done in or on water

**competitors**—those who are trying to win or do better than all others

**conversion table**—organized chart showing equivalent values in two or more units

**convert**—to change the form or unit of measure without changing the size or amount

**feats**—achievements

**hour**—units of time that are 60 minutes long and make up 24 equal parts of a day

**minutes**—units of time that are 60 seconds long

**records**—performances or achievements that are the best of their kind

**regiment**—a military unit that is usually made of several large groups of soldiers

**seconds**—units of time that make up 60 equal parts of a minute

**suspended**—to have hung something so that it is free on all sides except at the point of support

**time**—the attribute that is measured in minutes, seconds, hours, days, and years

**unit**—a set quantity used as a standard for measuring

# Index

Baumgartner, Felix, 22–23

Bog Standard, 10

Bolt, Usain, 6–7

Botwright, Jordan, 8–9

China, Edd, 4, 10–11

Concorde, 24–25

Erban, Mischo, 14–15

fastest commercial flight, 24–25

fastest electric skateboard, 14–15

fastest escape from a straitjacket underwater, 18–19

fastest escape from a straitjacket while suspended, 18–19

fastest sailing trip around the world, 16–17

fastest speed skydiver, 22–23

fastest toilet, 10–11

Furze, Colin, 10

Joyon, Francis, 17

Larsen, Owen, 8–9

Ledecky, Katie, 21

MacArthur, Ellen, 16–17, 26

Ohno, Apolo, 7

Phelps, Michael, 20, 26

piggyback racing, 4, 8–9

Rothacker, Alex, 12

Sweet Pea, 4, 12–13

Wilson, Lucas, 18–19

# Answer Key

## Let's Explore Math

**page 5:**

1. Minutes; Hopping on one leg around a classroom only takes minutes.
2. Seconds; Writing a name only takes seconds.

**page 9:**

1. 671 seconds; 11 × 60 = 660; 660 + 11 = 671
2. 657 seconds; 10 × 60 = 600; 600 + 57 = 657

**page 13:**

1. Day 2: 5,100 sec.; Day 3: 70 min.
2. Seconds; 60 sec. = 1 min.; 60 min. = 1 hr.; 3,600 sec. = 1 hr.

**page 15:**

1. 1 mile per minute; 60 ÷ 60 = 1
2. 12:15; Number line should show jumps equal to 150 minutes, or 2 hours and 30 minutes, between 12:15 and 2:45.

**page 25:**

2,173,000 meters per hour; 2,173 × 1,000 = 2,173,000

## Problem Solving

1. 360 hours; 3,600 ÷ 2 = 1,800; 1,800 ÷ 5 = 360
2. 408 hours; 2 days = 48 hours; 360 + 48 = 408
3. 180 hours; 1,800 ÷ 10 = 180
4. 438 hours; 18 × 24 = 432; 432 + 6 = 438